R.C. Basner's collection of elegiac poems remembers with the fidelity of art. This is mature work, marked by breath-taking use of the forms of poetry, its traditions, its technē as well as its ethos. Inscribed to poets, physicians, musicians, and artists, his poems summon haunted presences and absences to come. Some of those mourned were killed in the Holocaust, igniting rage along with grief. Although the poet is himself a physician, these are not poems "about" medicine but rather poems that emerge from the doctor's inevitable grief regarding the nearness to death and the ultimate futility of impulses to heal. We welcome this powerful poetic voice, speaking at once the tongues of body, soul, and spirit.

Rita Charon, Columbia University

Given Robert Basner's distinguished background in medicine it is no surprise that this work is so expertly and exactly crafted. The rich and precise choices, delivered, yes, surgically, carry us with sensitivity and humility to the important places. This is fine, fine work and it is to be savored carefully. As carefully as it was created. I am better from reading it. Consider it. Receive it. Enjoy it.

Phillip X Levine, Poetry Editor, *Chronogram* Magazine; President, Woodstock Poetry Society

Robert Basner's poems are full of mystery and music. We must work hard at plumbing the depths of the sonorous poems of this latter-day Gerard Manley Hopkins, but we are the wiser for it. Archibald MacLeish famously wrote, "A poem should not mean, but be," and Basner's poems *are*, in all their rich complexity, in their tragic and cryptic beauty. He never lets us off the hook by providing meaning or morals. Rather, he lets us see the world through his own sad, wise, brilliant doctor's eyes. As elsewhere in *For Medicine, Memoriam*, Basner doesn't let us look away in "Church and Majestic" : ("…I know now when next we speak/ will be in the abiologic-/void our voices can have no touch in./ But mine will tend towards yours."). The consolation Basner offers is in his unique vision and in the exquisite delicacy of his words.

   Elizabeth J. Coleman, Editor, *Here; Poems for the Planet* (Copper Canyon Press, 2019)

Medicine. Nature. Music. Three realms where sentimentality hides what's truly valuable. In taut and compressed language that eschews any easy meanings Robert Basner's poems please the ear as well as the intellect. He brings a physician's incisive wisdom to bear on the most important elements of life, such as mortality, illness, faith, kinship, fate, art, and poetry. His own poetry is thrilling to behold.

   Will Nixon, author of *If Not In Heaven, Then In Saugerties* (Bushwhack Books, 2024)

Renowned physician, composer, and musician Robert Basner finds his rightful place in the tradition of Chekhov and William Carlos Williams with his first poetry collection, *For Medicine, Memoriam*. Wielding language with a conductor's brio and surgeon's precision, the poet beguiles with musical and innovative word play. In spare, masterful storytelling,

Basner brings a sensory beauty and spiritual mystery to his powerful exploration of nature's mutability, death's inevitability, and personal loss.

Licia Hahn, Associate Fellow, Berkeley College, Yale University; Founding Member, The Poetry Annex

This is an adventurous first book of poems by a senior physician who has encountered a wide variety of memorial events. The poems merit close re-reading. Not afraid of using a "brutalled language" in which nouns and verbs exchange their customary rôles, Basner invents variations and new purposes for old words in "[a] life that is languaged." In this manner, a number of traditional subjects, the loss of friends, ekphrastic poems about artworks, and memories of places are distinctively refreshed.

Michael Salcman, retired neurosurgeon and art critic, editor *Poetry in Medicine, the anthology of medical poems*, author of *Shades & Graces* (winner Daniel Hoffman Book Prize, 2000) and *Crossing the Tape* (2024)

Robert C. Basner's poetry collection, *For Medicine, Memoriam,* is the debut of an exquisite poetic talent. His work combines a delicate sonic sensitivity with deftly original syntax that sounds almost like a language of its own: a language of beauty and elusive meaning that breaks linear expectations. Basner's poems also display a wealth of metric variation that seems as natural as his "quiet dialect of breathing."

Sharon Israel, author of *Voice Lessons* and host of the WIOX Radio Show/Podcast Planet Poet-Words in Space

For Medicine, Memoriam

Robert Charles Basner

SPUYTEN DUYVIL

New York City

ACKNOWLEDGEMENTS

An earlier version of "Physician's Pillow" was read as part of the author's 2023 invited address to the alumni convocation of the Columbia University Vagelos College of Physicians and Surgeons, and is video-archived there.

"For Ellsworth Kelly, His "Plant Drawings" was published in an earlier version in *Promethean*, Spring 2014.

"First Snow" was published in an earlier version in Lee Slonimsky's poetry collection "*Bright Yellow Buzz*," Spuyten Duyvil Press, 2022.

"Gulf Of Spezia" was read in an earlier version at the Keats-Shelley House in Rome, May 2019 by Lee Slonimsky as part of his talk entitled "John Keats and the Pythagorean/Petrarchan Sonnet." It is archived there.

"In Memoriam" was published in an earlier version in *Chronogram*, January 2023.

The sculpture on the title page, "Ballerina," is by Stuart Hellman, photographed by the author, and is printed with Mr. Hellman's gracious permission.

Marianne, Emily, Leah

Contents

III.   *The Piano Tuner*

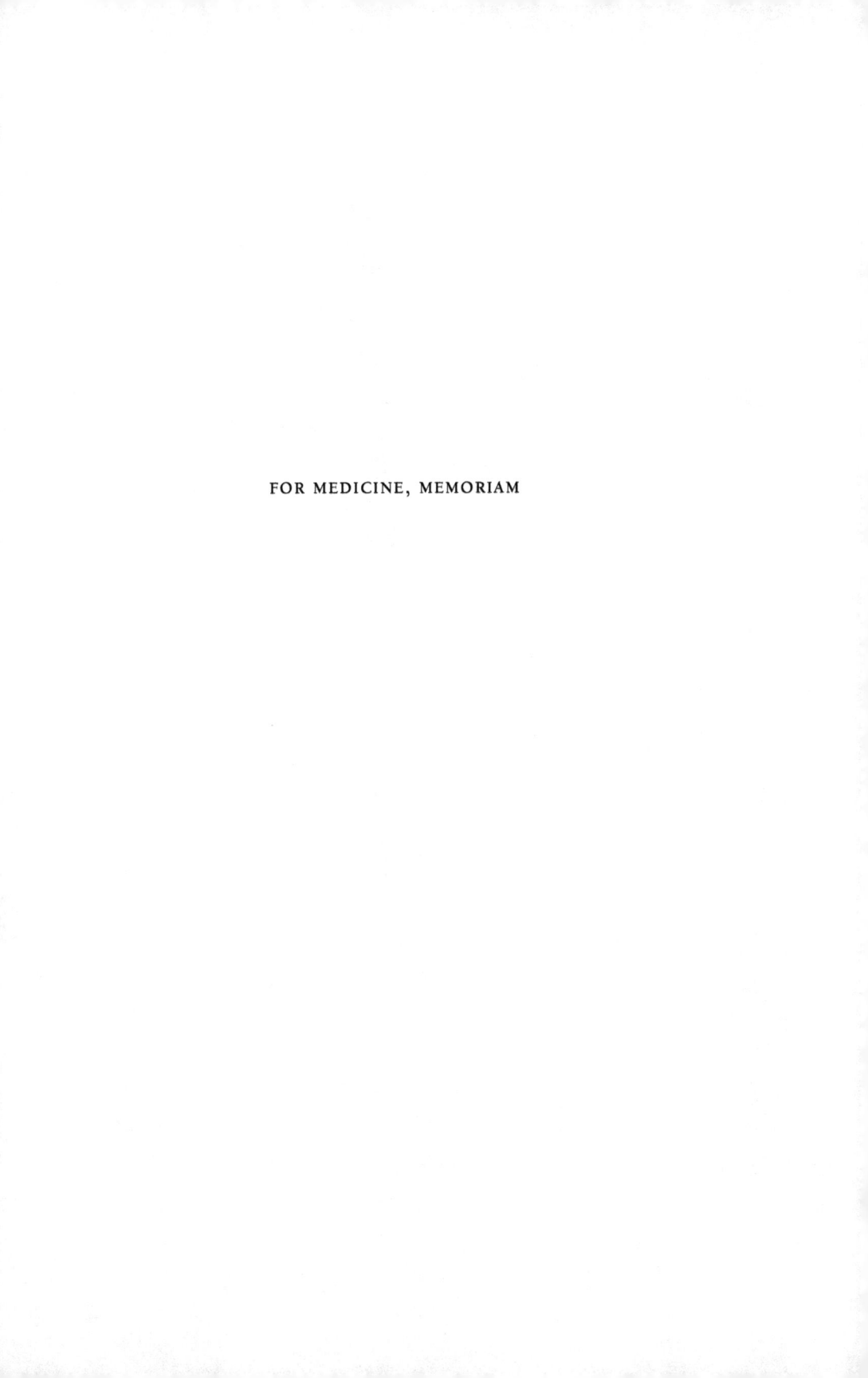

FOR MEDICINE, MEMORIAM

Foreword

Not since William Carlos Williams published his first collection of poems in 1909 has there been a more auspicious debut volume by an American poet/physician than Robert Basner's *For Medicine, Memoriam*. Resemblances between these two poets' work present themselves in ways well beyond their professions: a symbolism filled with electricity, images etched with a painter's eye, and startling line structures, for three. And Basner's work has a stunning originality all its own, as can be seen in the conclusion to one gem of a poem, "Sempervirens": "...In cold coast fog's/foliaging, its height the forgetting of forest; its/evergreen the light that is left in lonely things."

Intense and lifelong reading of all poetry can be detected in this amazing collection: for example, a subtle echo of Frost in "the light that is left in lonely things" above. The syntactic swerves of Hopkins, the terse and sudden beauty (like flower petals unexpectedly opening) of Dickinson are also present continuously.

In Basner's compelling poems, a truly original American voice emerges. It's one in which the pen is wielded with the memory of the scalpel; astute and artful scholarship of both surgery and syntax appear behind the poet's painterly eye; and the poet's composerly harmony of sound is heard profoundly.

Another tradition to which Basner's debut creates a stunning addition is that of American Jewish poetry, diverse in its various sensibilities as the work of Ginsberg and Reznikoff, Hollander, Kumin and Shapiro. This deep tradition is united in its cultural (if not always religious) heritage. Basner's own consciousness regarding the Holocaust, for one example, grieves profoundly, always with traces of religious awareness, yet questioning. The unforgettable, searingly brilliant line:

"Even the tips of the wails on the Western Wall at times seem to touch blue" ("At Times") resonates with an imagistic hope of a poet who is also a beautifully deep thinker.

Basner's profound and immortally beautiful perspective will change the life of any reader who spends time with his inimitable poems.

LEE SLONIMSKY
AUTHOR OF "PYTHAGORAS IN LOVE"

IN AN ATHENS
BOOKSHOP WINDOW

THE CRITICAL CONSULTS OF POETRY
—in memoriam, Paul Oppenheimer

The critical consults of poetry will
never have consummation accurate
as medicine's, whose prognoses must
prove bitterest biology; never as

accurate as landscape's, whose
lecterns must be lamped in limitless
late; never will have consummation
accurate as war's, whose wounds must

be wished; never accurate as Law's,
which levies immortal Liable. The
critical consults of poetry, as medicine's,
as landscape's, as war's, as the Law's,

will never have consummation accurate
as music's: God's accuracy.

In An Athens Bookshop Window

—in memoriam, Konstantinos Lardas

—"and the word was made flesh, and dwelt among us"

Now enough plague's pane is sun
to see sea pity in it; see

wasped webs and rosed cold cobble
cover plain tabled pages their

poets have passed from poorly, for
even Asclepius's art has

grown too feeble for word poised,
warred paused, scalpel; and as

for the poets, cease's own saying—
of a beloved, of April, of Athens—

had long since been posed.

FOR MEDICINE, MEMORIAM

— for Ralph Blume, M.D.

Breath on bone, but who terrored trust
against me scathed beneath sworn
scalpel held with my mistaking for biologic,
belief; mistaking breathing for compelled:
graver scathe, even, than God's, who has
mistaken for aged, ashen; for medicine,
memoriam.

PHYSICIAN'S PILLOW

Now mine, but many heads have been
held on this hospital pillow's elite

launder: on it, I hear my father,
when I was son here, gasping kindly to

his father gasping kindly to his
father. On it, I hear my first patient,

when I was student here, bleeding into
his brainstem; I hear his eyes widening

with each heartbeat emptying him: and
there began the art of finding how to

phrase final when heal is not to be.
I hear on this pillow my last patient,

when I was Professor here, whose
breathing had become "that of a person

recollecting himself" after his heart's rare
ravage. On it I hear my protégé 's

protégé lecture at the bedside on the
subject of my doom, not noticing

my eyes are sometimes open. Doctor,
the greater we grow at diagnosis,

the graver is its guise: surprise attends in
death-decided eyes.

The pillow is pulled from my head. But
you hear me, daughter? You hear, the

gasping gone, me pleading kindly to
my father? But I will never say

how these poems, my prescriptions;
these prescriptions, my poems, must

be bound into the volume with which
burial might be borne.

Daylilies

The ill, too, are as fever amidst mid-
summer's day, accomplishing bloom

shrubbed in afterbloom; common color
against peeling porches whose whites

clutch at belonging along rural routes
rutted in arrival the ill, too, route return to.

How We, Who Are Well-Versed, Wear Our White Coats

How we, who are well-versed, wear our white coats?—
in exhaustion's nightmares, as when

we rushed to her gurney, so young a
woman, whose brain's especially spidered

fibers were torn with bursts of blood,
webbed with clots of what's called "stroke."

We dream our dread—as when
each blow of blood against her brain was our-

selves hammering precisely weighted
instruments at her head, heaving skull blows:

we thought the first enough to be her
end, but had we stopped after the first, or even

second, hammer blow, she might have, yet,
survived; but we went on beating her head,

where she was only infant fontanelle,
until fatal was finally struck, though her eyes

stayed, still, open, on us, —sadly?—her stricken
breath still beauty. Morning, from drains we

had expertly drilled into her skull to relieve
her pressured brain's imagining, leaked her

sickened spinal fluid, that crusted gold
halo around her head on her softening

pillow, and with ghosts groping for her pulse,
she stopped breathing. Bur her eyes stayed

staring, now at her children, now at us, and her
mouth was moved into smile—to be beyond it?—

How we wear our white coats? I hear disdain, or
worse, a lazy muster to wear your own. We,

well-versed, in empty corridors sleeve our white
coats white-stained with what was wished.

LAST DAY OF AUGUST

Twenty? A third of the length of you,
who lengths in chases of chestnut hair,

is jewelled— half is, when you lean forward. Your
dress flowers a mountain town. Now you

turn, and half hold a latte for your customer;
twice saying my name, twice seeing past me,

who had asked your eyes, and then your mouth,
for that latte not ten minutes ago. And have I

done something wrong? I have lain with just
such a young beauty as you, in just such a mountain

town, breathing her breath of summer's sweet
humidity, and you have lain: it's just that I have

been in such love fifty summers more. So. Though
I thought ageing would never allow the eyes to age,

the unwarming latte you hold glancing with summer's
uncertain is latte seared in summer certainty.

November End

If not for Malevolence—that
vile ridding God of role—here

would be mere of melodic;
fragrance fragment; barning

of red in Maple while wintering
white in Pine; most of mourning.

And passing of this poem would
be poem.

In The Surgical Theater

*—"The ability to defy the natural order of life and
    death made Asclepius both revered and feared…"*

"You have no more right to this child,
surgically draped, antiseptically stiffened

under your scalpel, who has just
bypassed, alone, her blood and breath, a

desperate death in your own Time's
sparse stint in surgical theater. You have

no more right to reverence, while your
hands—formed so formal as can escape

art—have left open the failed wound,
while her corpuscles still ooze through

it for air; while hope still waits in the
corridors. Let your best student not

allow the alarmed cardiograph and
ventilator, but pull the stinging sterile

taped tube from the thin throat; let her
put almost sweet sponge to the stick

mucus frothed from the mouth and, in
the hiss of cold surges of surgical theater

that no other mortal must hear, taut
almost tender the stitch of neither faith

nor fathom, but that could hold, in heal,
the next heart diagnosed as Donor. For

until now, you were not the one to bear
beings in discreate; the bodies of those

who were to be, so soon, unbeloved.
But bear now Simpler; the poetry that

medicine swears to imagine."

In The "Natural Burial Ground"

Mound, but no more a grave than
is any ungreen. What has gone into

it is no more of beloved than maple,
though under maple as much as

may be; no more of reached for than
rain on it is reached for, though

under, as much as may be, a rain. How
may we, when we must, measure

such indifference? How is found
intend to such untend?

Hospitium

The lab coat is left hanging in
the closet, its pockets sealed

with a worn stethoscope and
prescriptions; its white cloth still

clung to the punishment of chest
that endured each of the un-

endurable deaths; each of those
lives reminds their loss in it.

Packed are the few brief belongings
that this gasping into its own airways

allows. As I leave, I expect from
the hospital no more than I expect

from the grave: the care of corridors
hiatused with the unhealed in coffin

light; the glint and glance of stethoscope
and scalpel not studious enough. I

expect from the hospital no more
than I expect from this poem, or any

other's urgent elegy: a diagnosis, or
a missed diagnosis.

Villiers-sur-Morin

—after a watercolor by Jacob Barosin

"…the rural places, the trees, are unwilling to teach me anything…"

Abandoned villa; violet Villiers-sur-Morin;
sun you've painted the sides of it with is

its why. The seated of the few of you left in
the doorway is the quiet dialect of breathing

that is just before being found below warned
windows warmer, roughened roofs roser,

than was allowed;

is the quiet of droned slow cicada and
bee hum of color that could have been a

summer, but that you were brought to it
by your own brutalled language: already

there was the rifle-battered deportation to
be; the agreed to of agony's inhale; your

cracked yellow corpse fumbled off bodies
beneath you of older hope. I held it, your

time: a thin paper of colored waters, and
meant to move its remembering to a safer

place, but my poem, too, has ended with
words different than what I had written,

though yours is the life that is languaged;
the language of violent quiet, still, of an

ageless afternoon in villaed Villiers-sur-

Morin.

Tilt

To boy-height eyes, tilt was wide on a
kitchen's unfinished floorboards to

a north window's summer morning,
unsunned, sill wasps droning cold

over webs, and the green of almost black
ashade, ashake, on a stone fence's ferned-

further; on a sensed to-be of summer's lilt.
Norther now, there's surprise in surprise that

age's raze was so sudden that the stones that
have stayed of the fence are sunned now, not

only windowless and woods-less, but weather-
less; and tilt was always to its only distance.

No Longer Landscape

SPOKEN IN OCTOBER, TO BE HEARD IN JANUARY

—after Andrew Wyeth's "Snow Flurries"

If I allowed poem
into my landscapes,

they would be no longer
landscape: they would

be worthless
work to passion

progress of
place, as though

fence posting fields
already under

flurries further than
forgotten assures

us ancience; or
ochreing as autumnal

what is already oak,
authors autumn.

"WEATHERSIDE" (1965)

Time gave up as quickly here as its
brushwork was finely given; but there

are presences: in the roof pitched for
pine air's sag and seep and dissolve,

its seem also of sea; in each window's
half waited-for weather; in ceasing sides

of cedar that could collapse in the least
lean of color. And a comfort: a clothes-

line angled into ashen, caring into
what has no distance of going.

SEMPERVIRENS

That T'ang poet, silence of sixteen centuries,
but by his own seasons already humbled; whose

Huangshan pine, as his poems, he hardly hoped
was homaged by a Heaven brushed by such

hardness of height and of lasting: would he have
been solaced by sempervirens? In cold coast fog's

foliaging, its height the forgetting of forest; its
evergreen the light that is left in lonely things.

In A Room With Two Rembrandt Intaglios

*("Landscape with Trees, Farm Buildings and a Tower," third state;
and "Christ Crucified Between the Two Thieves," fourth state)*

The rain brown of the room reaches
only the surfaces of these late prints'
prerogatives of pity. Yet there is such
harm. There is such hovel. A master,
in final state, has drawn over distance's
chance at Church, leaving that other
far that falls to embrace foliage and
face engraved in intricately ungraced
emptying.

CLEARING

It would not have begun
as burden, this clearing cut

into hilled woods, skilled
with the soil and sawn sweet

of a noon-day summer's
scent and hammers heard

only in noon-day summer's
distances. But dwell there

would be, always, about "a
weather coming in," much

of it cold; of sight-lines
hiding a small house's heft;

and much about shades long
after their suns, and in those

suns, the part of pine that limbs
windless motion; and in those

shades, what of such clearing
slopes away; what is sloped to.

Corot's Birches

If landscape mattered, it was
only intense seeming:
that clear things outlined coring
color could, as summer wished,
contrast with while. And if
the white of birches is ashen,
now, and always near an odd
and an old autumn; if old rose
is a color because of old rose,
it's clear each leaf of summer could
never be accounted for; each leaf
of spring never withstood: age has
allowed summer to have been
young in; art has allowed wisp of what
of summer must be, at last, left out.

At Times

With worship or without—for we are Jews—
this is land whose light always was to be learned

in loss; light in which even paralyzed eyes could
passion the patience of Torah. This was foretold.

This is as seems. But what if certain deaths are too
much mattered to agony for their after-souls to

ascend to serene? Even the tips of the wails on the
Western Wall at times seem to touch blue.

DRAGONFLY POND

—for Lee Slonimsky

Entrance cattails, sedges, unsummering
scent; geese, gone over wet waver, still voice

lengths away, but known as not returning.
The pond itself one of summer's small waters

at edges, no motion of its morning but for a
drying dragonfly floating, wings twitching to

any left amaze; to any penitence of a late place;
invisibly green of never wasted weather.

Along Nicasio Valley Road

(West Marin County)

Pacific, too, possible suddenly poorer:
how may summer here— its ocean cold

fog flows imagining rain onto redwooded
roofs all night until its wasted wet can

warm into wildfire flower and cherry
fragrance of morning— be deciphered

now as dear? Pacific, too, its drought-
steep, sun-stranged solitudes held in by

falls of fences, hilled that poses climb to
be in its distance but not its day.

Winter Clearing

That wasn't love ended,
that is ended,

when summer so
surely was ended: each

tree we'd known;
each reach of their

rustle you sshushed,
in lengths of chestnut hair,

now found in frigid thins
of year's end: that wasn't

love ended. It wasn't love
ended, that is ended, when

builders, breakfasted,
flannelled, dieselled, had

gashed with winter plough
their own clearing, wide white

and gray gravelled roadway,
without a sense of where the

weather was, before the foot-
fearing ground would become

too frozen to bury a doorway and
its distances deared not just

by our dead, but by your eyes.
And your eyes? They should

have been spoken of sooner.
When they first hazelled and hayed

without me, no, that wasn't
love ended,

though it was rended, then,
and is ended.

"Gulf of Spezia"

—"The tall, slight figure, the jacket, the volume of Aeschylus in one pocket, and Keats's poems in the other, doubled back, as if the reader, in the act of reading, had hastily thrust it away, were all too familiar to me to leave a doubt in my mind that this mutilated corpse was any other than Shelley's—"

Paint Spezia? Summon summer to splurge dry brown
brush tips: rose redded whites; cypressed; housed; hilled;

and any wind or whorl there, well. Such summary of
summer; such mastery of what is meant by exquisite. But

Spezia is also a place so simple of seaward as to be drown.
You must have held, before you painted, your brush to what

was also exquisite here: a poet's last hope of morning
pigments dreading in a violent violet face, once heretic, now

haughty with hauling unsaving sail, unfleshing in mud
dredge what must be meant of ebb, of time, mouthed

in the torn coat pocket's mould.

RUIN

Even pogrom was worded in *t'shuvah*,
for our dead, for our youth,
when we fled forgiveness to farm
here. Here, also, were errors of earth,
but if we were too poor for our own poems,
we worked, at least, weather's. If those
are known now as rain pooling passing;
as a wagon's weed wheels sunk in sun
gusts where wildness flowers, they've
spoken rust to rose: you speak ruin of
another's language; a grieving longer
than gone.

For Ellsworth Kelly, His "Plant Drawings"

—on the opening of his 2012
exhibition at the Metropolitan Museum of Art

Leaf line vies with
bare space,

versed stems
flown, then flourished:

the graphite gathers
green, but

these leaves are
loose, too,

and framed so,
ache of acres'

falling foliage
in bare place,

which too is
bloom.

NOTICE

To take notice that an amateur
attempt at sun in a water-

color of cold that is New
England just after noon

mid-winter, in wind that
pleads to no near person or pine

than void there violetted, is the
predictable part of that kind

of cold,

is to take notice that aged itself
is in amateur ajar to where the light

has been falling from, and to
whom, has been falling.

View Of The Csobánka Countryside, April 20, 1942

— after a watercolor by George Byfield

How those hills could unfold a
lifetime in an accurate palette of

 first month of spring viewed
from contagion's contempt for

such caring? It is what any
April is greened with in our going;

what daffodils sun's last matters. It
is what is sensed as saved for lilac;

it is what attempts the un-agony of
hands left lain in unused purple,

white of poorest paper; it is make-
shift of morning as is any art.

"Winter Landscape With Fisherman"

— after a painting of that title by Shi Zhong
(late 15th-early 16th century)

Because the fisherman sits unsurprised by
precise of six centuries' brushwork, in rain straw

clothes, snow boughed, snow bowed, snow wised
by a village's precipice, he is assumed in midsts no

weather would bear, or be: the snow has
fallen more adrift than that, fallen quieter than that.

CRAB APPLE TREE, SULLIVAN COUNTY

In the unowned brown photograph
of an almost autumn fifty years

before us, we could see that, were
we there, we would be fifty

summers too late. Now, our own fifty
more summers and a day later,

what alones the sun splintering an
old crab apple tree is no longer summer:

what exceptional light must have fallen
to see the tree against pasts when what

was whispered under its reaches was
already boughed wrong to the road;

to see that we are now to be seen in
the brown, still unowned, photograph.

"Last Poems"

*"...the survival of many of his poems (some
hidden in saucepans and old shoes, some preserved
because his wife, Nadezhda, had learnt them by
heart) is something of a miracle."*

Sun sheer, for the first time
uncertain of its weather; a

tense saucepan and a tired
overturn of shoes places to hide

poems: in Voronezh, I have no
certainty of soup; in heart failure,

I'm not allowed even my wayless
walk. Landscape was my early

exile—first poems—but here is
exile without landscape: last poems,

to be so named, not by their time
written, nor their time read—nor by

any tyrant's time—but by time that she
who has heard them by heart has gone on in.

"Beech, Godshill Church Behind...July 25"

—*"Sweet especial rural scene."*

Whereas your words, wild's while,
trespassed the terribly tolled

meanings at weather's edges,
your summer's sketch was more mortal,

your pencil gaunt's guest, that lifted
leaves toward beech-shaped solitudes to

lapse by what the loss of you would leaf,
in lifted, there.

VILLAGE GREEN

—in memoriam, Thomas Patrick Boyle, M.D.: Tom

On sun green, greener patches
of sway of shade of pine, and oak, and ash,

that if left uncrossed in summer's reach
will be left uncrossed at summer's last,

when light is learned in leaf for each
leaf-long light passed.

Author Photograph

—with reference to Andrew Wyeth's tempera "Trodden Weed" (1951)

Death would be someday between
your "author photograph" and the

worth of your words that wished
your weathers there; your time of

wool coat and plaid collar stopped
in brutal brawl above your smile—

your eyes, or mine, the poorer
translator? If not for that painter's

intricately trod boots a child
withers his father in, your own

self-portrait might have been missed:
an old master not staring out in art,

but staggering from it.

First Snow

— in memoriam, Marie Ponsot, who reminisced that, while she had spent many summers of her youth on the farm, she had never stayed through to winter.

"O fortunatas nimium, sua si bonanorint, agricolas"

First snowfall always fit,
Being already bare:
war's thought, as thaw's, in it,

that tanks would plough the cold in it,
cursing farmer to warrior:
first snowfall always fit.

As white as feels falling of it,
it will lay gray on late faces lain there:
war's thought, as thaw's, in it.

For grief or sweet of it,
this was always abandoned air:
first snowfall always fit.

Reapless as the rain that ends in it,
for this is too ancient an air:
war's thought, as thaw's, in it,

that leaving always fit,
though summer itself were there.
First snowfall always fit,
war's thought, as thaw's, in it.

MEASURE

There are poems that have no need, now,
to have been made. But here, where a
mist of rain glazed gray photographs
a road that no longer has a roadside, but
has November, an emerge of a few glint
green cawed-cold globes of crab apples
from branches brokenest brown is one
of death's miracles of measure—as is aging's
aging of hand, once held here, held here.

SIGN

Never has been such unconvince of
sip at a cardboard coffee cup when

standing on the gravel of a Sunday rural
roadside stand's afternoon; never, of

August's goods, or good, or goals, or
farmed, or gardened. Never has been

such confine of mauve in chrysanthemum;
never such stranding of sun's sense of

summer on never-since as that on this warped,
unpracticed-paint lettered sign: "*Buy, Swap,*

or Sell" half-hidden by its own fade, half by
its fall to fern's unhinge. Never, such ungiven of

green; never summer itself the homelessness
for each sought settling in.

At Length

Grotesque, in a graveyard,
to assume anamnesis—which

is, that is, weather—that is,
aloneness—or, at least,

ramshackle—which is, at the
least, wind trying to be trees

trying to be lost, or, at least,
at length—which is—that is—

at last.

Claude Monet, Age 86, Studies His "Le Bateau-Atelier," Painted At Age 34

Circumstance spring, he could
concern wayless with wake

in lengths of light of the
little enough that is lilac and blue

to lunge and lull a water to
deeply morning. Circumstance

summer, he could concern himself
with whether wake had been

made with weather enough to wane;
whether the length of light

would be enough to leave depict
dissolved into depicted.

No Longer Landscape

Who knows that the light is July as
July light lays over? It is summer-

September's acrid accurate
to answer in unveil of vista, and

its voices that gather in
voiceless rooms, gone attentive, to

decide the dead. It is summer-September's
to be silent, that is no longer landscape,

for it has an age now, and an edge:
it is my age; my edge.

THE PIANO TUNER

"A Viola, Barcelona, 1779"
(inscribed "Filius Fecit")

—from an auction catalogue

Great maker's son made it,
lateness already lyric

in its rare lathe and
graven ground,

when death decided my
own child, her rarer ear

bowing bow's grief to the
worn warm of it,

would waver her eternal
brief from its bound;

and bid distanter music:
the lost, or beautiful,

become of
other's mourn.

THE PIANO TUNER

Shabby smile shtetl
shares, hands his own old,

still meant maestro
shrugs to tune my shambled

piano. Tones he has
long since trued to

perpetuity he tries
again, but each touch

is alone in harsh harmonics—
an aged ear cast into an

aged cortex. Now, in the frayed
fingers of air he passages

an old music remembered
as rare ravish, but hears no

key to context God, chord,
or cadence. Pity? but

isn't this master compose:
dissonance of dear—

gaunt, or gracefully, got—
to have heart's heave

exact?— to have rehearsed
its unaccompany?

"Quam Olim d:C"

Then stricken, he envied his
own elegy; but who is so soprano

now, to be the mortal of his choired,
meant to conclude his covenant—

not with the agedness of the God
of Abraham— but with the agedness

of music: to be his command that votive
voices pass, to be, again, beginning?

"In Memoriam"
—in memoriam, Lionel

Jagged; justly inscribed, but
even rare written is word

interring word: those that
bereaved us meant us music,

whose grief is abandoned grief;
whose resonances are unresolved:

in stricter airs they rose
remembering languageless.

Church And Majestic

So summers-begunned; so
summer's attics unstaired; so

summer's shutters shuttered; so
in summer's shades unsured;

so summers-worded with half-
waited; so illed with summers-ended

I never saw, I know now when next
we speak will be in the abiologic—

void our voices can have no touch in.
But mine will tend towards yours.

Against Amber

Autumnal build of beams above already
high windows, against whose glown amber

of always some other latening of afternoon,
umbered red gritted leaves stain. Inside,

it must be, are art's attempted warmths.
But of outside, the careful of caulk and

clapboard was always, to common color
become too cold to consider sustenance,

coward; each abrupt air's
roughenings of pine, always reason.

"The Decent And Devout People Of Ys"

—after the piano prelude "La Cathédrale Engloutie"
of Claude Debussy, 1910

You hold us the "decent and devout
people of Ys" whose drown was music;
maestro imagined. We appear
arpeggio? Buoyed by your pious assessment
of poured chords? Our dread was just after
our drown; on your piano, we've left the music
left, only octaves: the music of drowned music.

"Airborne"

—after Andrew Wyeth's 1996 tempera of that name

—"When the work was next seen publicly in October 2001…the composition had changed. The artist had taken the panel back to the studio and added more feathers flying in the open sky."

A day always
known but not
before been:

gray degrees; must-
mauve of soon to
be snow;

brown chants chancing
at pond reeds, their
pauce pulled at

by ice pooled in
paused amaranthine
and on unheard

windows; above grass
dutiful green of
darken

found by a fining
of feathers
flown falling from

their geese's
frozen going
early in

the painting.
The young
live in the such

of such
unpersoned
day; the old live

in the day itself,
uneased, in
cedared eaves'

unseen sea'd
silences. Excess
of art acclaimed

when first
exhibited,
the painting's

older poet has
breathed brush
to five more

exacting falls
of feather—
aging in fresh phrases

for passing
passed;
for unknown

weather
vaned to a
violet

whitening
of bounds
of borne;

for end
unlike
itself.

Assume The Mourned

Assume the mourned are
mourning, though they mask

no mirrors; though they
have no seven, or thirty,

days. Your own soon-
enough-to-be mourned

exacts enough extol for the
distance between last breath

and the breath dearly not
taken. Assume the mourned

no silence, though seems
their silence: their old can't be

older than music, though they
hear hard keyboard.

A Radio In The Catskills

She calls from sleep: "wake now and
put the cones back on the pines, the

lilac back on the branches"—but that
was only groaning of once green on

glassed frost fragments of moon—
and morning, its constancy of cold

uncovered on winter where-d roads, was
me, who must rely for living voice on

rural radio waves that only the barrening
of leaves summer was saving allows

reach of dial's distances this far into
the mountains. Still, its faceless wars are

mostly static: shrieks in shellfire, whose
children will never need death to protect

their aging; fading Parsifal spells; an hour
of pleased-with poetry. I'm listening for

the poem whose music interprets its
word withered words.

"Kaddish For Solo Violin"

—of Gideon Klein, 1919-1945

The hands
of the violinist

at the cloud
narrowed,

curt colored
1918 Nice window

were as known to
undestined death

as the hands that
would care horror's

violin from its case,
ashed in Auschwitz; and,

in rose amber rosin
scented sound,

grotesquely holy,
allow its composer, again,

unendurable end,
that he might ask his

wrought: "you had
wrest; your mar I

meant, pieced with palest-
purposed pitches to

stun your bearers
with the beautiful of

what won't be—the rest
refused—but had you gift?"

PARE

Agreed, disregard it,
its once more of

weather; blossom only
because of brailed paper's

receipt for watercolor.
Sun-in-wind-white,

rain-rush-plummish,
precise sketch scarlet-

pare: beauty only
because of careless, and

flair of passing into itself.

In A Mountain Town

Bid summer go, as once you bade
when bade could become an autumn. Or
has your bitterer bade already been

borne in the gait of one going from wan
warm to wan wished, colder than those
colors, not hearing his goings as gone?

PIANIST

"It was too slow because you conducted it too slow."

Who knows piano knows death—
that startle of exquisite chord
change we hear as summer; that
grace of haggard hesitance of
voice before enthrall in choral-
all; that cadence flawed as flaws
the unfamiliar a first phrasing
perseveres.

NOTES

For Medicine, Memoriam:

—"aged": meant to be pronounced as a trochee.

In An Athens Bookshop Window:

—The epigraph is quoted from *John,1:14, KJV.*

—"Asclepius's art": in both Greek and Roman mythology, Asclepius was god of medicine and healing; he was likely, too, a war surgeon. In such mythology, he was slain by Zeus, at the bidding of Hades, who feared his skills in medicine would allow him to bring the dead back to life, thus rendering humans immortal. See also below, the notes for "In The Surgical Theater."

Physician's Pillow:

—The words, "like that of a person recollecting himself" are ascribed to a Hippocratic physician attending a dying patient by Francis Adams in *"The Genuine Works of Hippocrates"*, vol. i. p. 371. London, 1849. The phrase describes the patient's breathing pattern.

In The Surgical Theater:

—The epigraph is quoted from Evangelia Hatzitsinidou, in *"Asclepius: The Divine Healer of Ancient Greece"*. On-line, Olympioi.com, August 22, 2023.

—The second epigraph is from Act V Scene II of *Hamlet*.

Villiers-sur Morin:

—After a watercolor by the artist Jacob Barozin, in the United States Holocaust Memorial Museum Collection. The painter survived the Shoah; the events of the poem are purely as imagined by the author.

— The epigraph is a translation from Plato's *"Phaedrus"*.

"Weatherside" (1965):

—After Andrew Wyeth's tempera of that name.

In A Room With Two Rembrandt Intaglios:

—Regarding the later state of the Master's print *"Landscape with Trees, Farm Buildings and a Tower"*: "The cupola has been removed from the tower and the area of foul biting in the sky completely cleaned." From the exhibition catalogue *"Rembrandt: Experimental Etcher"*, copyright 1969 by the Museum of Fine Arts, Boston, Mass.

At Times:

—"learned": pronounced with two syllables.

"Gulf Of Spezia":

—After Henry Roderick Newman's oil painting *"Gulf of Spezia"* which hangs in the Museum of Fine Arts, Boston.

—The epigraph is quoted from Edward John Trelawny, his" *Records of Shelley, Byron, and the Author;"* the Penguin English Library, published April 1983.

For Ellsworth Kelly, His "Plant Drawings"

—"foliage" meant to be pronounced as a dactyl.

View Of The Csobánka **Countryside, April 20, 1942:**

—After a watercolor by George Byfield depicting a Nazi-allied Hungarian army forced labor camp; the painting is in the collection of the United States Holocaust Memorial Museum.

Last Poems:

—The epigraph is quoted from the preface, by James Greene, of his volume of translations, *"Osip Mandelstam,"* Shambhala Publications, Inc., 1977.

"Beech, Godshill Church Behind…July 25":

—The quoted title is part of what was written by Gerard Manley Hopkins on his pencil sketch.

—The epigraph is quoted from his "Binsey Poplars."

First Snow:

—The epigraph is from Virgil, Book II of the *Georgics.*

"A Viola, Barcelona, 1779":

—"bowing:" as bending in reverence; "bow's:" of that which is drawn across the viola's gut strings.

"Quam Olim d:C"

—The title quotes what are considered to be Mozart's last written words, his notation in the score of the *Requiem KV 626* to repeat the fugal section "Quam olim Abrahae promisisti" of the *Offertorium*.

"The Decent And Devout People Of Ys":

—The title and quoted part of the text are from Sudip Bose, *"Out of the Watery Depths. Debussy's Sunken Cathedral."* The American Scholar, June 8, 2017, as below:

"Only the cathedral, symbol of the decent and devout people of Ys, enjoys any kind of afterlife, as it is said to rise up out of the watery depths on clear days at sunrise, the ringing bells and booming organ audible across the expanse of the bay, before sinking back into the sea by night."

"Airborne"(*1996*):

—The epigraph is quoted from Karen Baumgartner, in *"Andrew Wyeth People and Places"*, 2017 by Skira Rizzoli publications, Inc.

A Radio In The Catskills:

— Based on the phenomenon of foliage's attenuation of radio waves.

"Kaddish For Solo Violin":

—"The hands of the violinist…"—a reference to Henri Matisse's painting, *"The Violinist at the Window, 1918."*

—Gideon Klein, who composed "Kaddish for Solo Violin" at Terezín, died in Auschwitz.

Pianist:

—The epigraph is quoted from Maestro Fritz Jahoda, whose passing was in 2008.

ROBERT CHARLES BASNER, M.D., Emeritus Professor of Medicine of Columbia University, is heir to the farms, fields, foliages, and fervents of place slipping shyly, forever, off the Catskill Mountains. An Alpha-Omega-Alpha graduate of the Columbia University College of Physicians and Surgeons, he continues teaching in the Department of Medicine at the Columbia University Irving Medical Center as a Special Lecturer in Medicine. He also holds a Bachelor of Music degree from the City College of New York, where he studied composition and conducting. This is his first collection of poems.